A Quick-Start Preparation & On-Boarding Guide for Work-at-Home Solo-Entrepreneurs

Straight-to-the-point foundational guide for the beginner solo-entrepreneur starting an independent business from home.

ISBN-13: 978-1514608302

ISBN-10: 1514608308

Published by: Createspace

CONTENT

DEDICATION

~~~Dedicated to all the solo-entrepreneurs who are striving to start their own independent businesses.

My heart felt desire and vision is that all achieve their destiny in starting and growing their phenomenal businesses that they so richly deserve. ~~~

Introduction

"You are ready to be your own boss but let's face it working-at-home could be a bit challenging."

Hello!

Congratulations! You have decided to pursue your dream as an entrepreneur—specifically a Solo-Entrepreneur and an independent business owner. You will be starting your business from home while working part-time/full-time or maybe you quitted your job or experienced a layoff and your desires to be a solo-entrepreneur is in high gear and you feel the joy of the luxuries of working from home is now or never....*Wait!* Perhaps there is a hint of uncertainty you may have working from home?

Are you truly ready to embark on this path to starting your independent business by working at home? Sure, it's great not to have someone tell you when to start or leave. No restrictions on lunch breaks or restrictive vacation time. What a lovely experience not having to have those Monday morning 8:00am meetings or <u>forced</u> to work overtime.

As a solo-entrepreneur you will be embarking in new territories in managing your business that you would never imagined. You have researched, trained, studied other entrepreneurs and now you are ready to claim your status as a solo-entrepreneur....*Or are you ready*?

You might experience feelings of confusion, frustrations, isolation and a host of other gushing feelings that is all part of the transitioning stages for a solo-entrepreneur business. This process takes time and it's great to put together a system that will work for you to ease into the process of running an independent business.

What Is This E-Guide About?

I am providing this E-Guide as a straight-to-the-point foundational information for beginner solo-entrepreneurs who are starting their own independent business and working from home. This E-Guide is <u>not</u> for those seeking advanced level information on advanced marketing or advanced selling or starting a business from a brick and mortar location.

This E-Guide will offer step by step basic points I provide in my solo-entrepreneur career coaching sessions about transitioning to solo-entrepreneurship such as establishing your business name, basics to setting up a website, free and simple social media marketing and how to effectively setup and operate your business from your home, that will motivate you to feeling like not just a solo-entrepreneur but as a CEO of your own independent business.

After many years in career coaching I have found that providing a simple step by step process to help career changers to solo-entrepreneurship helps build the foundation for running an independent business through understanding the preparation, foundation and the on-boarding process in setting up their independent business.

"A Quick Start Preparation & Onboarding Guide for Work-at-Home Solo-Entrepreneurs" is a foundational guide that was created for individuals who are solo-entrepreneurs working from the comfort of their own home. This quick-start guide's goal is to help you get started on the practical step by step work-at-home preparation processes for solo-entrepreneurs.

"The foundation is the beginning step before advancing to the next level of growing an independent business."

I want you to be able to:

- Be comfortable with *your* decision!

- Be mentally and physically prepares to run *your* business!

- Be excited with *your* new CEO/Solo-Entrepreneur path!

Cassaundra Wells

Chapter 1
Foundation

When a person decides to become a solo-entrepreneur the first thing one may do is determine the type of business and how to sell the products and services associated with the business. The process of perhaps going to trainings or reading massive amounts of books or online resources relating to starting a business is absolutely beneficial, but a lot of the researching, training, product buying, and networking can be a diversion from setting up the foundational piece in solo-entrepreneurship.

A potential home owner who longs for buying his or her first home spends time shopping for furniture, ideal outdoor lighting and buying that dream patio set. There is nothing wrong with window shopping but he or she has not even applied and obtained approval for a loan to even begin looking for a house. The potential home owner has not even completed a home buying seminar. What is the hold up? Fear of commitment? Location? Is it that the person wants to become a homeowner has not spent time thinking about what it means to transition to a home owner?

The above situation can happen just as well with any solo-entrepreneur starting an independent business from home. The preparation to work at home involves preparing mentally and physically along with establishing your own on-boarding system as part of your foundation to effectively and efficiently work from home.

I have focused on six areas that I consider the overall focus of this e-guide:

- ➤ Where/How to Start
- ➤ Foundational Understanding
- ➤ Areas of Preparation
- ➤ Your Own On-boarding System
- ➤ Knowing Your Business Structure
- ➤ The Office Transition

Chapter 2
Preparing the Mind

<u>Mental Preparation</u>

The mental preparation is understanding as much of the pros and cons to becoming a solo-entrepreneur that can affect your mental preparation for the transition. Ask yourself these questions:

> ➢ How long did it take you to decide on the type of business?

> ➢ How many times did you start and stop your business?

> ➢ How many times did you talk yourself to starting your business because you thought it was "not the right time?"

> ➢ Did you seek other people's opinions if you should start a business?

> ➢ How many times did you use the "money" issue for a reason for not starting?

> ➢ How many times did you convince yourself that you need to conduct more research or need more training?

> ➢ Will you be bothered that your family or friends may not understand or be immediately supportive?

These are just a few reasons or excuses that can be conjured in a solo-entrepreneur's mind that while these may be justifiable to some, it can equally be self-sabotaging the mental readiness to becoming a solo-entrepreneur. The hard part is actually accepting the benefits of starting your own business. The easy part is thinking of cons of starting a business because of fear of such things as the instability of income in the beginning or you may not have the support that you thought you would have.

Very early on you realize that you are in it alone as the "lone-wolf" solo-entrepreneur. In this mental state, you'd want to be able to move from questioning whether being a solo-entrepreneur is your calling and to mentally move towards an absolute destiny of acceptance on your decision to be a solo-entrepreneur.

Chapter 3
Preparing for Acceptance

Acceptance Phase

Acceptance is the second important phase in the mental preparation. Uncertainty of income, where and how to find clients, accountability to yourself are just a few areas that you will need to accept as a solo-entrepreneur. Even if you are starting your business around your day job, you still have to mentally accept that you are running a business.

Let's begin by removing the terms "side-hustle, side-jobs, side-business" and any other reference that you are working your business as a "side_." Consider the fact that if you think of your business as a "side-hustle" you will most likely be operating your business as a side-hustle. You get to it when you can. When you don't want to be bothered you walk away just like a relationship you are trying to avoid.

That is what your customers are going to do and they will treat you and your business as a side-hustle and will buy products from you on a whim. Ask yourself why do people need to know that you are operating your business as part-time or "on the side"? This is what many solo-entrepreneurs do that sabotage their branding and growing their business. The power of words plant the seed in other people. If you speak and promote your business with words that plant in a potential customer's mind which causes a customer to treat you unserious or as a "side-hustle," you will find yourself frustrated and possible give up on your business.

No one need's to know you are running your business part-time or around your day job. The hours are just numbers on a clock. Your marketing should not have any subliminal messaging sort of that speaks that you are operating as part-time or as a side job. Don't fall into the trap that you feel you need to justify when and how you are operating your business.

I want you take note that wealthy people have an enterprise of multiple businesses. I assure you wealthy people are not thinking part-time or side hustle. Mentally accept that you can run your business in the hours you know you can commit. Do not self-sabotage yourself by telling people your business is a part-time hustle unless you want to be known as a side hustler of businesses.

Chapter 4
Preparing the Body

Stress Management

Working for yourself definitely has a lot of perks. But as solo-entrepreneurs, we definitely are not isolated from the stresses of running a business even from home. Working from home a solo-entrepreneur has the pressures of running the front and back office operations of one's business. Even with a few people assisting you in your business, the feeling of total control may take over because you know exactly what you need done and exactly how you want it done.

This is why it is important to develop a specific work schedule that includes breaks and lunches. Who says you can't take a two hour lunch? Use this time to exercise, plan a real lunch with friends (away from home) or a quiet lunch time with yourself. Whatever your heart desires just be sure do it. However, if you know you will abuse that two hour lunch that turns into a four hour waste of time, then refocus and modify either your time frame or what you do with your time.

Managing stress is not easy for everyone but achievable with the right motivation. I keep saying that while you are assuring that others don't take advantage of you, be sure not to abuse yourself which could cause you both physical and emotional stress.

Chapter 5
Access Your Time Management Skills

<u>Time Management</u>

I am sure you have an idea of the importance of time management in your daily life. And now that you are running a business from home, you will be busy doing the things that would normally take a team of workers to complete.

I want to share with you some *time management tips* that will help you establish a system of routines and consistencies in your daily schedule to help you work efficiently and hopefully avoid melt down and ciaos.

Tip #1: Create a business binder that will serve as a visual system to an organized workflow at your fingertips. Divide your binder that will have all of your main areas/divisions of your business that you will need to focus on right away (i.e. Payroll, invoicing, marketing, goals, conferences etc.). Include a calendar and additional pertinent information that will save you time from having to pull out excessive papers and files. This is your daily go-to binder.

Tip #2: Use a calendar to plan and keep track of activities and appointments. I recommend utilizing at least a hard copy general calendar for your business binder, google calendar, and portable appointment book.

Tip #3: Specify work hours for yourself and stick to it. Set about 15 minutes to wrap up your day reviewing your appointment, reflecting on what you did or did not accomplish and make out your to-do list for tomorrow and walk away until tomorrow.

Tip #4: Set aside a day or two during the week to <u>not</u> focus on business. This will give you time to reflect on your personal time and the energy to focus on your business with a fresh mindset and positivity.

Tip #5: Be a realist and try not to feel you have to do everything immediately. In the beginning, you will have trials and errors in your time management strategy. Once you start seeing that to-do-list of activities forming to a consistency, you will begin developing a system that works for you in your scheduling.

Tip #6: Set order in your home with family and friends because some people will not appreciate your time because you are working at home. Set boundaries with family and friends and let them know you are working and keep to your work hours.

Tip #7: Social media can be time consuming and must be planned. Planning your social media posting strategies is a part of your weekly planning schedule. Be consistent and block out any distractions.

Tip #8: Prioritize your to-do list of items. Writing things down will help you stay focused and keep your schedule organized.

Tip #9: Keep all of your business and networking contacts in a centralized location in your business binder have an electronic copy. Why do you need to boot up your computer or look for your phone when you can flip open your business binder to get this information? Think of practical and quick access to information.

Tip #10: Avoid bad habits by valuing your time and don't take for granted the minor tasks that are just as important in running your business efficiently. Try not to get discouraged by things that don't quite come together immediately. As weeks come and go you will continue to self-reflect on what is or is not working and make the necessary adjustments.

Chapter 6
Financial Management

As a solo-entrepreneur you may be already uneasy knowing that your income will be up and down until your season of consistent growth. It is very important to monitor every incoming and outgoing of both your personal and business expenses on a weekly basis down to every penny.

Having a busy month or months may not necessarily mean you are profiting especially if you have to still spend money on additional essentials for the business or playing catch up with overdue bills.

To monitor your comings and goings of finances, you definitely have to keep a separate filing system for your accounting needs. To do this here are a few tips to managing your business finances:

1. If necessary, hire an accountant
2. Learn about proper tax deductions especially home office deductions
3. Invest in the proper accounting software or manual paper trail
4. Keep good records and all of your receipts
5. Prepare a budget of projected expenses
6. Be firm and specific on payment due and invoicing from your customers and clients

Keep in mind that every penny counts. Things like subscriptions, webinars, conferences, business cards, marketing flyers, computer paper and ink can add up very quickly.

Protect your urge from commingling your personal and business funds by opening a separate business account as soon as possible. You will be forced to work off your business budget and preferable not touching your personal accounts.

Chapter 7
Establish Your Business

Think about what kind of impression you want to leave on others? How do you want to brand yourself and your business? Now that you have transitioned to an independent business owner, you have the luxury of building your own brand and reputation.

I want to state that a business can be promoted to build a brand around a person's name such as a well-known professional speaker or comedian. Also a business brand could be built based upon the type of service (consulting services) or products (3D Triple Blue Custom T-Shirts). This is something you have to think about especially if you have a few employees now or will be adding staff down the line, having in mind that the concept of the business may change. You would also want your staff to understand your business.

A quick-start to getting started in establishing your business takes a few careful ideas, planning and strategies to get you going to build your business. From creating a business name to establishing a functional working environment, all these will help you transition mentally and physically to feel like a CEO of your own business.

Naming Your Business

Establishing a business name is a part of the integration process. A business name addresses the question "Who are you or what do you do?" Naming your business is actually the fun part in starting a business (in my opinion).

Creating the perfect name for our business sets the tone for branding of your business. Think of this process as a way of connecting with the public. Building a reputation through the use of the website involves careful development, but I encourage you to be as creative as your heart desires, so you do not take away the professionalism you want your website to present.

When thinking of a business name think about the services you are offering. For example, if your business is motivational speaking and you are branding yourself as a national speaker, you may prefer to be known by your name. So in this case, your domain name would have your name (e.g. johndoe.com). Apply the same scenario assuming you want to create a consulting business. So your business name for branding could be (johndoeconsulting.com).

"Keep in mind that you have to always conduct a check to see if your domain name is available and if your state requires you to check with your city/municipality assuming you are required to register your business." The best place to start is going to IRS.GOV or state's government website for more information.

- ## Business Structure Status

Simply, I'd recommend going to the IRS.gov website to review the explanations of the different business classifications (Sole-Owner, LLC, Corporation etc.) and how you decide to set up your business affects your tax liability and registration in your city/municipality.

- ## Employer Identification Number (EIN)

Applying for an EIN is fairly simple and can be done online through the IRS.gov site. There are circumstances that determine if you are required to apply for an EIN right away. An EIN may be necessary depending on how you wish to set up your business structure status. An EIN is often needed to set up business bank accounts including what is called "doing business as (DBA)" accounts.

*"I recommend reviewing IRS.gov and/or consulting with your tax attorney/accountant for detailed information."

Setting Up Your Website/Domain

Your website is an electronic business card that can be seen by everyone. A website is for attracting customers to your business. You are a reflection of your business, so you'd want a website that exhibits professionalism. Creating a professional website does not have to be a grueling process for those of you that are beginners.

Creating a domain name to attract the right attention can be fairly simple. You will find online suggestions on how to formulate a near perfect domain name for your website. Depending on the length of your business name your domain name may have to be slightly different from your business name but the domain should be a reflection of your business.

How to start: write down a few ideas for your domain as you would like others to see it on the website. I'd recommend at least two or three options. Once you have selected a few names, you'd want to go online and do google search to see if there are any existing domains matching your selection.

Once you have selected a potential domain name, you will then have to register your domain name with a host provider to register to create your website. As an additional perk many hosts offer at least one free email and depending on the hosting plan, additional email accounts may be included.

I'd recommend googling and searching top website hosting sites and comparing their plans to fit your initial budget. In most cases you will be able to upgrade anytime during your plan.

Be advised that there are two options for setting up a domain with a hosting provider:

- **Option #1:** domain name chosen will have either the host site name included for free (johndoeconsulting.weebly.com).

- **Options #2:** domain name does not have the host site as part of your domain but there is small fee based upon the hosting site fee plan options.

Web site Builder Options

There are many website builder/hosting options to choose from that varies in hosting prices. I personally went through several years changing my website host because my needs changed. Not all website hosts will offer the same features.

If you are new to creating a website, then I'd recommend starting with a free plan or a plan that has a free trial or a low cost starter offer for 30 days. If you are pretty savvy on a website as a result of having experience setting up a blog/website for yourself or someone else, then you will probably focus on cost and features.

For the beginners that never created a blog/website or the computer savvy type, don't worry. A few hosting sites such as Vistaprint, Homestead, Weebly has ready-made templates or theme options. There is a lot to choose from and I have found out that these particular hosts are very user friendly.

Another widely known website host is WordPress. The catch with WordPress is that they are very particular on certain features you can use. Note that there are wordpress.com and wordpress.org.

- *Wordpress.com*-free publishing platform with both free and cost theme page templates. The free themes do not allow for a lot of additional perks such as adding plugins or you may not be able to sign up your website as an affiliate.

- *Wordpress.org*-You have to find a separate hosting site such as GoDaddy, HostGator Blue Host etc. There is a lot more involved in setting up and managing the site. Great for those not afraid of a little grunt work and/or want more features.

Establishing Your Social Media Account

Using the internet to build an online presence is just as important and almost a necessity. LinkedIn, Twitter, Instagram, Google+ and Facebook are the most common social media venues that are used for personal and business purposes. These are free basic accounts to promote your business.

The main benefit of using social media is to increase visibility of your business nationally and internationally. Social media has the ability to connect with individuals that can refer your services and establish new customers. Every post you make about your business has a potential customer.

There are a great deal to learn about social media network options. Unless you know someone that is social media savvy, time is needed to get familiar with other social media networks that will work best for your business.

- <u>Social Media Management Tools</u>

<u>Hootsuite:</u> Allows you to manage and post to multiple social media accounts. The cost varies from free to a small monthly fee. I recommend starting with the free version and you could always upgrade at a later time.

<u>Bitly:</u> Main purpose is to shorten links for posts to social media accounts. There are other features. However, the most common usage is for the basic purposes of link shortening.

<u>Buffer:</u> Social media scheduling and sharing content to your social media accounts.

"These are just a few suggestions for social media management tools. I recommend googling for additional options that will benefit your business needs."

Office Equipment

While you are getting started, the last thing you may be thinking about is spending money on a big ticket office equipment right up front. There are cost effective methods you can use to obtain a few equipment that won't break your budget.

Tip #1: Ask friends or family if they can check with others if anyone has a gently used laptop, iPad, Tablet or Computer they want to donate. If you have actually started a non-profit, then the donation could be tax deductible.

Tip #2: If a special day such as a birthday or mother's or father's day is coming up for your gift, ask for a small monetary gift or indicate how you would love to have a laptop or tablet.

Tip #3: Check with a few schools in your area if they are in the process of upgrading their computer system or have old computers that they donate to families.

Optional "FREE" Phone Services

Skype:

This Basic *FREE* service is usually for making calls to other Skype account holder. It is great for conference calls especially if you have assistants who also work from home.

Skype also allows you to communicate online via messaging. Cross between texting and emailing.

If you need to make calls to a non-Skype phone number then you do have an option to sign up for a basic Skype calling plan that includes international options. Skype's plans are very reasonable and much less than basic cell phone bill. You can choose the number and if you want to pay for multiple numbers, that option is also available.

You can have multiple Skype accounts, but you will have to have multiple usernames that is required when creating an account.

Free accounts do not qualify for a free Skype number, but the very low cost for a monthly subscription or annual subscription is worth purchasing when you have determined how Skype can be effective in your business.

Google Voice:

Quick and easy to set-up, plus it's FREE. You will need to establish a Gmail account and have an active cell phone or landline. This option will allow you to make calls from your Gmail site. You will also have an option to have calls routed to your alternate phone that you provided at setup.

800.com Toll Free:

Do you think you would need a toll free number? No problem. I personally favor this site because there are options at the time of writing this guide that is composed of five options that range from pay as you go to under $50 a month plan.

The drawback to some people is that the pay as you go plan does not offer 1-800 but offers other toll free numbers. I personally have searched online for various companies that do not have the traditional 800 number, I have not found them any less credible and I personally have not had any problems or concerns from my clients. I do provide both the toll free number and my local contact number on my website and correspondences.

This service also includes fax by email as part of the monthly plan—available for all options. If you have never faxed by email, you will have to scan your files and save to your file folders and then login to your 800.com account to fax.

Chapter 8
On-Boarding Process

This chapter involves the creation of your very own on-boarding process for your business. An on-boarding process is much like an orientation and on-boarding process for new employees at a new job to introduce them to the company. Establishing an on-boarding process is viable especially when you decide to grow your staff.

Think back on the first day of your job. How was your first day? Do you ever think back wishing that you were shown more or there should have been more involved in getting you acclimated into the company?

For some companies there may be both a formal employee orientation and a specific structured on-boarding process of the new employee. The employee orientation may involve finalizing the new hire paperwork and then a brief company overview and policies. Then the new employee checks off that he/she attended the orientation and then was sent on his/her way to the department he/she was assigned to work.

What happens after the orientation is then the on-boarding process. The employee is integrated among the co-workers. The process of the integration could take a few months or longer depending on the size of the company.

For example, an employee's first week involves getting acclimated with new employee orientation, meeting key staff, scheduled meetings, trainings, assignment of desk/office, getting supplies and someone from the I.T. department setting up your computer and access information. The next 90 days will involve getting acclimated with other staff, the culture, learning to not only do one's own job but learning about the company's structure.

Now that you will be working at home you now have to think like a business owner and operate as a business owner. As a solo-entrepreneur, you are the CEO, COO, 1-person board member, public relations, human resources, payroll, marketing, supply clerk and the administrative assistant. You have to create your own check list of things that you need to set up at home to function as the solo worker in your business.

Ask yourself these few simple solo-entrepreneur on-boarding check list questions that addresses *"what happens after I hire myself?"*

1. What are the things that a new worker working for my company needs to know?
2. Who are my immediate contacts?
3. How do I feel connected to the company?
4. What is the company's structure?

The goal of your on-boarding system should be to quickly get up to speed in the operation and *integration* in your OWN business. There is nothing more uncomfortable than having that "new employee" feeling in your _own_ business. Also, creating your own on-boarding system will be viable when you are in a position to hire additional support staff.

Know the Back-Office of Your Business

Identify areas of your business by creating a business structure diagram. You may have seen this as an employee that shows a company's list of departments and key leaders.

Creating your business structure diagram helps identify the different areas of your business so that you can clearly understand that your business is more than just selling a product or service even when you have areas in your business that need to be addressed which normally would be attended to by other employees.

On the next page is an example of a Direct Sales Cosmetic Consultant business structure diagram for Lady Jane Doe for her business LJD Enterprise. Even though in the public she is marketing and selling products as an independent distributor. She is still running a business as a business. In this case on paper she creates an internal business LJD Enterprise.

I want to show that seeing your various areas of your business will help you to identify and understand how to strategize the growth of your business. Don't mind the SmartArt shapes I used, I actually have a hand draft of my business structure in my business binder and an electronic copy.

Day to day, if Lady Jane is emailing, mailing or physically handing out catalogs one is going to assume that there are no specific target audience. Over time, if Traci realizes that her women buyers are primarily interested in makeup and nail polishes, then her diagram will have a specific box for makeup and nail products. From there, Traci's marketing strategies will be adjusted to that specific product category(s).

The example areas that I have displayed is only a short list to give you some idea on how I recommend breaking down visually pertinent areas of your business. This business structure diagram works with all CEO entrepreneurs. The objective is to see in detail how your business is going to bring in profits and to understand what helps your business operate.

Take a look at the marketing area in Lady Jane's business structure diagram. Marketing is a broad area and should be broken into specific areas that you want and need to focus on regarding your business growth.

"Quick Tip"

As you are planning your business growth strategy, think like a CEO. CEO's have their business structure at hand and have the appropriate staff attending to the various operational functions of the company. However, in this case you as the solo-entrepreneur is handling all the different areas of your business until you are ready to build a team for additional support.

Lady Jane Doe: EXIM Beauty Advisor & Sales Consultant

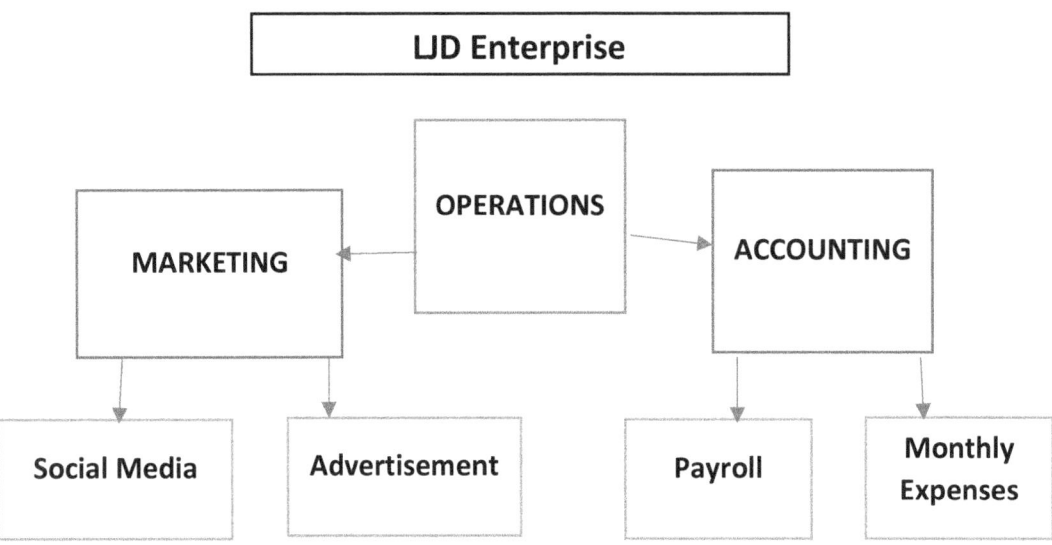

Now, take the same scenario and visualize Lady Jane having another business as an author. She writes "how to" books relating to makeup applications for women and she also designs women's jewelry. In all, Lady Jane has three businesses that bring her multiple streams of income. Lady Jane would include this in her business structure because she is actively working on all three businesses in LJD Enterprise.

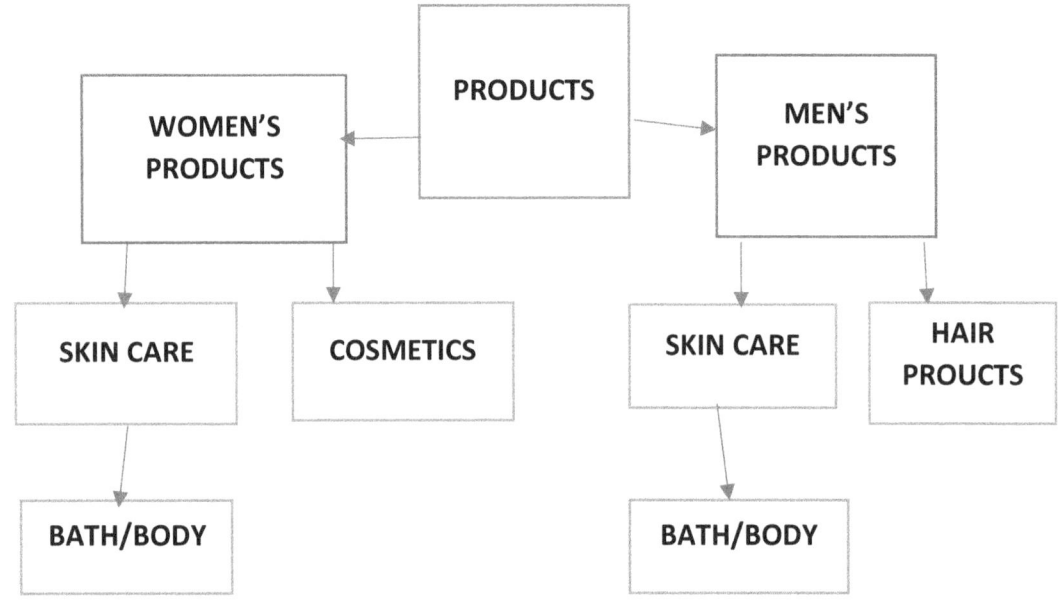

CEO-Business Binder Manual

<u>CEO-Business Binder</u> (3 ring binder): This will be your daily business binder of reference. I will say that there a lot of creative business planning kits that you can order online that have nice templates for such things as calendars, profit planning goals and creating your mini vision board. I am about simplicity and while these tools can be helpful, you could find yourself in a trap to purchasing items that may not fit to your needs or can only be used once to get you to order more products.

Start simple by creating your own personal business CEO binder. You will want to create a business binder that will stay on your desk or with your portable file box if you are utilizing a mobile office kit. In this binder, I'd recommend having the following tabbed sections and I will go into detail for the purpose of these sections:

- Expense Calendar
- Outline of Business Structure
- Daily Check List
- Notebook/Loose Leaf Paper
- Goal Sheet-weekly/monthly/year
- Business Plan
- Monthly Expense Calendar budget
- Conferences
- Trainings
- Social Media Accounts
- Policies/Procedures
- Contacts (business, vendors,)

Expense Calendar

Utilize a universal monthly due date calendar to make note of monthly expenses that include both household and business expenses. You don't have to download or buy a calendar. I prefer a blank calendar and I just fill in the dates. I found that keeping this in my business binder helps to see my entire monthly obligations and to stay on a budget.

I am aware of various bookkeeping software and I am all up for them. But instead of having to turn on the computer, I still recommend having items on paper for quicker access and still upload the information to your bookkeeping system.

Departments/Division

I mentioned earlier the importance of understanding the different departments or divisions that make up your business. Each area has a different purpose that requires a different area of focus. This is why a daily check list would be helpful. For instance, should you focus on marketing hair care products or focus on marketing skin care products for the upcoming quarter?

Daily Duty Check List

The same way make a list of your "to do" items so that you do not forget what needs to be done or make a grocery list of items in order not to overspend applies to your business. Make a list of not only what you need to do relating to your business but as well make a list of all of your personal appointments.
If you were working for someone else, you would typically schedule personal appointments several weeks or months out in advance to give enough time to schedule time off. Even though you don't have to do this when you are self-employed, you'd still want to try to at least make note of all personal activities that may interfere with your business plan for the week.

Don't overlook the importance of your day to day business tasks because you may be tempted to feel that there are minor tasks that can be pushed aside to the next day which will eventually turn into a few weeks or a few months. Be careful not to take advantage of what is perceived as minor when it's the minor things that could be just as valuable to the growth of your business.

Business Plan

Don't be afraid that this is not going to be as technical or deep as you may think you have to create. This business plan will identify the short-term and long-term goals for your business. In your mind you know what you need to make it financially, but to achieve this goal you have to take baby steps and plan out a strategy.

I assure you that your initial business plan is not the "catch all" plans. Things will change especially if you are not seeing the profits that you desire. Two objectives for a business plan:

1. Mapping out an action plan for achieving your goals
2. Forcing you to know what is happening with the growth of your business in the present and in the future.

Goal Sheet-weekly/monthly/yearly

When you review your business binder you plan your daily, weekly, monthly activities and obligations. These goals are not only about revenues but as well as other areas of your business that affects your business.

Goals don't have to be so big to make them go far out of reason, but the goals should mostly focus on the immediate and short-term actions that is a necessary to your business. These includes increasing social media advertising by posting three-four blogs a week or obtaining five new vendors every month for six months.

If you routinely establish your target goals, you will be forced to establish deadlines and keep track of what is or not working. Gradually you will see how your short-term goals affects the outcome of your long-term goals.

Vendor List

Even though you may be utilizing an electronic record keeping software, I still recommend having some form of a hard copy of all of your vendors and their contact information including specifically, if there is a separate contact person for invoicing. You can still transfer the information to your computer. This comes in handy to view everything without having to turn on the computer every time to look up this information and especially if you have an assistant that does not have access to your electronic files.

Conferences/Trainings

A perk to being self-employed involves finding opportunities to attend local or out of state trainings or conferences that is beneficial to your business. Depending on your affiliation with any organizations or if you are an independent business owner under a national organization, you may have access to discounted trainings.

You want to keep track of these types of conferences and trainings for future reference and to use these conferences and trainings as a great source for networking (also may count as a tax deduction-*ask your accountant*). Also don't forget the online webinars that you attend. Keeping a list of the speakers is a great way in going back to do an in-depth research about their specialties for additional resources.

Social Media Networking Sites

As you create social media networking accounts keep a hardcopy master list in your binder. Social media sites is not limited to Facebook, Twitter, Instagram, and LinkedIn. Use Google to research different types of social media sites and even check on a few online article. You will find many of these articles that has a "share" button that will show a whole list of other social media sites that may be of interest for your business.

As you progress in identifying the best social media networking sites you will want to keep track of your sites and if you find out that you will need to assign your social media tasks to another person, you'll have a good running list of information to pass on.

Policy & Procedures

I am a firm believer in seeing is believing. This is a great idea to create in the early stages of your business set up. Focus on creating information that is immediately relevant to legal consequences either on you (business), client and customers that you could be sued in court and/or need to provide proof. Such as cancellation policy, refund policies, malpractice insurance submissions, breach of contract disclosures etc.

Contacts

This section is strictly for business contacts (not vendors) of viable names, phone numbers, email, social media, websites and anything that you will most likely reference as important to your business. For example, who is the person or company that will fix your computer or laptop? Another example is even though John Que is the CEO of XXE Company but Mary Que is the primary contact and she prefers not be contacted by her cell number.

What is nice, is this sheet(s) is a portable list that you can take on to other appointments or meetings so that if you want to pass on a contact information to another business partner, you will have all of the correct information at your fingertips.

Finally, as you learn about new business tools and learning what and how you want to focus on your business, your CEO business binder will most likely change a little or a lot. Treat this binder as your personal operations manual of reference.

Chapter 9
Physical Transition-Home Office Workplace

<u>Home Office Transition for Success</u>

I remember many years ago when I obtained my real estate sales license and excitedly signed up with a large agency with fantastic sales training. I did exactly what I was told to do after my first day of training. I sat on my couch or in my reclining chair and made my list of 30 names that I contacted to let them know I was a real estate agent and then I mailed out my business cards to the same 30 contacts with a personalized written letter.

Several weeks of how to sale, how to follow up on leads and convert leads to clients but I think back how I came home each day not feeling on the inside that I was running my business within a business. I sat on my couch reading my training notes and material trying to figure out my next move.

Back then, nothing about the training coached me about how to set up a home office and to mentally prepare and operate as solo-entrepreneur in running a business within a business.

Consider these questions:

1. *Do you have a separate room work or will you have to work from your kitchen table?*
2. *Can you arrange to work in or create a comfortable workspace?*
3. *Can your space accommodate the equipment you will need?*
4. *How much of a distraction will you be exposed to (such as high traffic area, window view facing a busy street or too close to the refrigerator)?*
5. *Does your workspace have space for things like a filing cabinet or other furniture accessories that you want or need for your business?*

Establishing a Home Office Space

Having a dedicated home office or home office space is important but there are definitely challenges to setting up your space to allow you to be efficient, undistracted (as much as possible) and most importantly, productive.

You'd want to set up a space to work that will help you focus on your daily tasks and to operate mentally as a business owner. You may not have customers or clients in this initial stage. However, you'd want to prepare set the mood that will motivate you to think and work seriously as a CEO of your own business.

Having a dedicated and consistent space to work will help with distractions, establish consistent place to work and respect those from clients that will have to come to your home for appointments. Be aware that others you live with may not take your work seriously. You will have to ask others to be respectful of your time as you will also be respectful of theirs. Just because you can talk or take breaks anytime your working friends may not have that luxury.

When you sit down in your office space you want to feel ready and excited that you are running a business you have been dreaming to accomplish. You want to have everything around you as you would when you were or currently sitting as an employee with your own cubicle space or personal office.

Creating a Positive Home Office Work Environment

Let's start with your desk space. Whether you are using a traditional office desk, kitchen table or you got creative and converted an old wooden door propped on two filing cabinets as your work desk, you want to create a free flowing workspace that will allow you to have an organized and efficient place to function.

Where is your computer positioned? If your desk is a corner style desk then your work and writing space may be more restrictive. You may have to add more filing cabinets or storage space to hold your files compared to having a rectangular length work desk or table where you may have more room on top for adding more necessary working accessories.

As you set up your work area you want to make a short list of things that you will need to get things accomplished practically. This short list is exactly what it is. A short list! There is a difference between wanting and needing. You may find yourself excited to walk into your local office supply store and go wild with buying things you really don't need right away.

Sample short list of non-office equipment items:

- Sticky Notes
- Notepads
- File Folders
- File Trays (2)
- Large 3 Ring Binder
- Sheet Protectors
- Tab Insert Sheets
- Calendar (hard copy, desktop and portable)
- Portable File Box with Organizer (with handle)
- Plastic Document File Case
- Filing Cabinet (optional)

Keep in mind you'd want a clutter-free zone in your work space. Every item you purchase has a purpose and a place. You want to make sure you implement a daily de-cluttering system. Incorporate a routine that 5-10 minutes before you "clock-out," you put everything in an organized manner for the next day so you can start with a fresh space.

Types of Home Office Spaces

I want to specifically identify that I believe there are three types of home office spaces that would be appropriate for different circumstances for those working from home.

Traditional Home Office Room

First is the traditional home office. This space is typically identified as a fully dedicated room where you would run your business. This type of room is for those that have extra room in their home such as a spare room, family/recreation room, loft or even a garage.

This is where you will have a table or desk, computer, fax machine, small, copier and a file cabinet. Later I will talk about incorporating psychology when decorating or decking out your home office space.

Portable Home Office Space for Work-At-Home

The second type of home office space is what I call the Portable Office for your home. This is ideal for individuals who do not have a separate room to set up a dedicated space away from other areas of the home. In the next section, I discuss how to set up a portable home office utilizing cost effective tools without the clutter and you will still be productive in your work.

The beauty of this type of home office is that a few of the suggestive items I recommend for your portable home office will serve as an asset for your mobile office for appointments outside your home office.

Mobile Home Office

Take what you need and go! Let me clarify that you will not need to take a box load of stuff unless you have items that you use for display to your clients. There are hundreds of mobile office kits that you can put together to fit your traveling needs that will keep you organized.

Home Office Entrepreneurs: Portable Office Space Alternative

Are you that person that has to works from the kitchen table or from the bedroom or both? I mentioned there are several types of home office spaces that included the idea of having a portable office for individuals who do not have the extra space for a traditional home office (room).

What I have found is that there is a lot of information on the internet such as YouTube, Pinterest and Instagram on how to set up and design a traditional home office rooms/spaces but not much detail on setting up a portable office.

The key for a portable home office is that you'd want to have the essential tools that can be easily accessible and that can be easily transportable. I have listed several tips on how to create a business friendly portable/mobile office kit.

Tip #1: You will want to purchase what I call a portable office business kit that has the following items:

1. Carrying File Box with Organizer (with handle)
2. 3 Ring Business Binder
3. Pen Case
4. Sticky Notes

Optional

1. Plastic Document File Case –I favor this as a must have for on-to-go appointments.
2. Laptop/iPad/Tablet
3. Laptop Cooling Pad/Desk

Tip #2: Your portable office can serve as a dual mobile office kit if you decide to work away from home. For example, at your local coffee shop or for your appointments. You can be as creative as you want to be for your mobile kit supplies. Just remember to keep it simple, organized and functional for your use.

Design Psychology of Home Office Spaces

What is Design Psychology and why is it important in the decorating or decking out your home office space? Simply, your surrounding can affect your mood and motivation which could affect your productivity. Think about it. Can you work looking at dirty walls? What about dark walls or looking at a blank wall all day?

Ask yourself what kind of home office environment will motivate you to get up early every morning and jump-start your creativity. Your home office space should be a reflection of you and your business. The beauty of having your own home office space is that you can be as creative as you want to be.

For example, if you have clients meeting with you at your home as a cosmetics consultant, your clients should be able see a display of your products, and if you are a fitness trainer, there is nothing wrong with using 2lb weights as paper weights. Again, be as creative as you want to be which will help in establishing a positive mood of productivity.

1. If you are operating with a portable home office space you can still design or deck out creatively (decorating your file box with your company's name or logo). Your business binder should have some display of your company's image, logo, mission or maybe a motivational phrase.

2. Whatever method you use to decorate or deck out either type of office space you have should have things that represent you and your business. From pens with funky colors or logos to your product displays decorating/decking out your office.

3. Even though you may not be meeting with clients at your home, looking at your surroundings on a daily basis draws attention as a reminder to your business which should motivate you to working your business with excitement.

4. To find creative home office space ideas there is a wealth of information on YouTube from traditional home offices, kitchen home offices, sunroom home offices and even converting closets to home offices. The options are endless.

Chapter 10
Optional Business Programs/Software Tools

If you have not already researched and bought the latest business software tools to help you with your business, you can definitely search online for suggestions and free trial offers. I advise to use extreme caution.

Don't buy because of the latest hype but do buy because of the practical use for you and your business. The drawbacks to using some software; is if you are not familiar with what you need then you may not know what to use. Also, if you are not as computer savvy, you may find that some of the software may be a little intimidating to learn.

The best way to see what online tools you will need is to do things the old fashion way—pen, paper and utilize the Microsoft apps you already have –Word and Excel. You can create your own templates that will cater for your needs.

Begin with looking at your Microsoft software components and the plan options. Typically the basic package includes: Word, Excel, Power Point and Outlook. Advanced options will include Publisher and One Note. Later, as you learn about other software programs, you can better judge what will be cost effective to purchase.

A few additional possible business programs and software tools that could be useful to research:

> Payroll/Accounting: Bookkeeping Software
> Online Appointment Setting: Scheduling Software
> Online Video Conferencing: GoTo Meeting
> Project Management: Basecamp

Chapter 11
Hiring Support Staff

If your desire is to add an additional help to your business in the very near future, then there are some things to consider when building up your team. There will come a point where you may need to delegate certain duties because you are either are not as skilled in a particular area. This is because wearing too many will not only affect your business but personal/family life.

I have listed just a few typical positions that could be viable for consideration when deciding what assistance you may need for your business:

- Accountant/Financial Coach
- Virtual Assistants
- Social Media Assistant
- Writers
- Personal Assistant
- Volunteers
- Freelancers/Independent Contractors
- Interns (paid or unpaid)

<u>Compensation:</u> There are several factors to consider when deciding to recruit for additional support for your business. I always recommend speaking with an accountant to discuss your options and tax advice pertaining to your business.

- <u>Contractor vs Employee status</u>- If you are not sure you want to deal with the burden of having formal employees, consider hiring independent contractors. Independent contractors are responsible for paying their own taxes and you issue a 1099 at the end of the tax year.

- You can find freelancers/independent contractors on freelance job boards, by contacting your friends and family and from social media networks.

- If you have never been an independent contractor or not sure of the proper paperwork needed to hire your own employee or contractor, definitely contact an accountant in addition to reviewing information found on the internet such as IRS.gov.

<u>Volunteers/Interns</u>-Using volunteers or interns (unpaid) is a great way to get additional support and it serves as an opportunity for others to gain additional experience. The drawback is that volunteers/Interns may not be as committed for a long period of time compared to someone who is compensated. I recommend choosing this method with caution and not just to "dump off" work.

Chapter 12
Avoid Information Overload Burn Out

I have to admit that this is not going to be easy especially if you love the internet. You want to learn as much as possible. From learning how to use social media to learning the latest technology gadgets that every business owner must have. This will definitely affect your time management schedule.

1. I recommend writing down what it is that you feel you need to learn first. Such as how to schedule multiple posts on twitter or how to place ads on Facebook.

2. Start with one or two areas you want to learn about and either schedule in your self-learning time as part of your weekly schedule or do this on your personal time.

3. Be mindful of information that promotes high income streams in a month.

4. Use caution when submitting your email to "free" online articles. This will automatically set up for automatic updates. You will definitely be bombarded with a multitude of emails until you unsubscribe.

5. Set up an email filtering folder to sort your emails. This way if you don't have time to read these emails, you can read them in your spare time.

6. There are a lot of online products that may or may not be beneficial to you or your business. Check whether the product is something you need right away or place it in your follow up file to review at a later time.

One More Thing
Suggestions for Marketing Your Business

Just a quick list of ideas to get you thinking outside the box on marketing strategies.

Trade/Vendor Shows

Check your local newspaper or contact any family members or friends that are in sales if they can inform you of upcoming vendor or trade show events. Also, I'd inquire about these events through your Facebook contacts.

Membership Associations

Search online for related associations or organizations that offer free or low cost membership subscriptions. You may have an opportunity to sign up to be listed in their professional directory for free or at a discounted cost.

Community Events/Festivals/Fairs

Google search online for city events for the entire year. Many of these festival/event (especially in the summer) have opportunities for individuals to pay for a vendor booth.

Schools/Child Care Centers

What school or child care center do you know could use the help with fundraising? Offer to sponsor a table to help with fundraising and in exchange ask if you will be allowed to display or giveaway a few free business products (e.g. pens, water bottles).

Webinars

If you love speaking this would be ideal without the worries for locating and paying for a hotel conference room just to have only two people to show up. You can pre-record or conduct live webinars.

Google Hangouts

Mainly this is a social/group conversation hangout. You have to have access to a computer or mobile device. What I've seen is that this not too formal of a meet-up session. The hangout sessions are a way to connect with like-minded individuals who share the same interest.

Your Own Workshops/Informational Sessions

You don't have to be a professional empowerment speaker to hold a workshop. Cater your sessions to a specific audience or general public. This is an opportunity to educate, train, coach, recruit and generate leads all while promoting your business.

Blog Site

If you create a website, add a blog page. Update your blog on the latest industry related trends, product updates and other relevant information to capture the attention of the public. As part of your marketing strategy you may select to post a link to your company's blog page several times a month. This will show readers that you are not just promoting the company's website to get people to buy a product or service.

Partner with "complementary" Professionals

This method involves connecting with professionals that compliments your business for referrals for services, and allows the opportunity to building a networking list. For instance, a fitness trainer can contact a nutrition coach to discuss collaboration to offer free seminars on fitness and nutrition for men and women over 40. Another example, a freelance photographer contact private wedding officiants to offer discount photography services to couples planning elopements.

Local Professional Chapters

Research in your city for professional chapters that you can join. Professional chapters often hold monthly or quarterly meetings which is an ideal place to network with existing and new chapter members. Many professional chapters may also have local or an online member's magazine that may offer advertisement services or "showcase" an article featuring a local business owner.

Email Links

When you set up our business email do not forget to add your business website in the signature of your email along with listing your social media network information.

"Every email you send out represents your company."

Fiverr

Fiverr is an online marketplace that offers various tasks and services at a low cost. Fiverr has what is called "gigs" that starts at $5 per gig. Depending on the intensity of the service you may be asked to contact online the gig worker for details. I've personally used this service several times for logos and editing. All the services I used turned out with great satisfaction.

Thank You

I hope this guide has given you the information to help your transition to solo-entrepreneurship and understand the preparation to working-at-home. I do personally understand that this can be an overwhelming experience, but once you get a system going for yourself, the rest will fall into place.

I wish you all the best on your journey in your business building and feel free to stop over at my Transformation Training & Consulting website or look me up on social media so we can connect.

Warm Regards!

Cassaundra Wells, MBA

About the Author

My name is Cassaundra Wells My mission.... (That I choose to accept) is helping others who are striving to achieve a new beginning to becoming solo-entrepreneurs or I like the term CEO-preneurs of their own independent business(s). Many whom I have coached just like you are coming to a conclusion that it's time to make a change and would like to know where to begin.

I have been in career coaching and recruitment for over 10 years. I have a passion for lifelong learning and empowering others through mentoring, teaching, career coaching and helping solo-entrepreneurs get on a path to self-fulfilling independence. I am the founder and CEO of **Transformation Training & Consulting** and **TT&C Employment Solutions.**

I have my Bachelor of Arts degree in Communication and a Master's degree in Business

Administration. I am an experienced college adjunct instructor in the focus area of teaching Social Psychology in The Workplace, Interpersonal Communication and Intercultural Communication. I am certified as a National Workforce Professional to provide career readiness coaching.

My 20+ year professional background has allowed me to obtain experience in customer service, facilitation, curriculum development, non-profit, human services, leadership administration, employment recruitment, personal consulting and career readiness coaching.

My moto that I live by: ~~~~ *"Mission.....Possible!"*

Cassaundra Wells

Cassaundra Wells, MBA
Transformation Training & Consulting
Website: www.careerprep4you.com
Twitter: @careerprep4u
Email: cawellsconsulting@gmail.com

www.ingramcontent.com/pod-product-compliance
Lightning Source LLC
Chambersburg PA
CBHW080651180526
45168CB00008B/3383